はしがき

　増え続ける自転車事故、自転車が加害者となる歩行者との衝突事故、前方を見ていても起こる事故、道路の曲がり角の死角での至近距離では歩行者に気づいても、避けることができないで起こる衝突事故、これらの自転車事故で加害者は重過失致死罪に問われたり、歩行者の被害者は脳挫傷、頭蓋骨骨折、後遺症などで、加害者は高額な賠償責任を負う。これらの事故原因には加害者の前方不注意などの判決で過失が問われるが、歩行者に自転車の存在を音で知らせれば事故を回避できるでしょう。

　自転車事故を回避する技術として、本書で解説する実用新案公報に記載されている権者（著者）の構成、鈴の音と反射板の光で、周囲に自転車の存在を知らせる技術の効果が事故例に対応する事故防止の使用を独創的に解説した。

編集部

Preface

There is a collision with the pedestrian from whom a bicycle serves as an assailant in the bicycle accident which continues increasing, by the point-blank range of the dead angle of the corner of a street of a road, even if it is seeing the front, even if it notices a pedestrian, there is an unavoidable collision and an assailant is accused of a serious mistake fatality crime in these bicycle accidents.

A pedestrian has brain contusion, a skull fracture, etc. and an assailant will undertake large sum obligation to pay reparations.

Although these causes of the accident are asked about negligence by judgment of an assailant's front carelessness etc., the accident will be avoidable if a pedestrian is told about existence of a bicycle to sound.

The effect of the technology of telling the circumference about existence of a bicycle explained creatively use of the accident prevention corresponding to the example of the accident with a rightful claimant's (author) composition, and the sound of a bell and the light of a reflective board indicated as technology of avoiding the bicycle accident by the industrial new design official report explained in this book.

目 次

1 自転車事故と過失責任の回避 ··· 7
　⑴ 歩道と車道の区別の無い道路、自転車と歩行者
　⑵ 二人乗り自転車と杖を突いた歩行者
　⑶ 車椅子と自転車
　⑷ 横断歩道の衝突、歩行者と自転車
　⑸ 曲がり角の死角、自転車と自転車
　⑹ 河川敷、ランナーと自転車

2 音と光で知らせる自転車事故防止の表現 ································· 13

5 公報解説 ·· 21

7 本書の奥付の発行№について ··· 47

8 過失責任軽減の主張マニュアルの案内

English description
Table of contents

3 ··· 14

Evasion of the bicycle accident and negligence responsibility

⑴

A road and a bicycle without distinction of a sidewalk and a driveway, and a pedestrian

⑵

The pedestrian who poked the two-seater bicycle and the cane

⑶

A wheelchair and a bicycle

⑷

A collision, pedestrian, and bicycle of a pedestrian crossing

⑸

The dead angle, bicycle, and bicycle of a corner of a street

⑹

A dry riverbed, a runner, and a bicycle

4 --20

Expression of bicycle accident prevention by sound and light

6 --33

Patent journal English

7 --47

About issue [of the colophon of this book] №

8

Guidance of the opinion manual of negligence responsibility mitigation

1　自転車事故と過失責任の回避

⑴　歩道と車道の区別の無い道路、自転車と歩行者

　　夜間自転車で走行中、歩行者の男性に衝突、衝突された男性の被害者は、意識が戻らない頭蓋骨骨折となった。自転車の加害者は、前方不注意の過失責任が問われる。しかし、この場合、自転車の存在を音で知らせていれば、歩行者は自転車が来ることを認識でき、自転車を避けて、事故を避けられるでしょう。

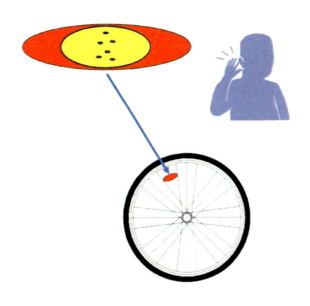

⑵　二人乗り自転車と杖を突いた歩行者

　　子供を自転車に乗せ、走行中、散歩中の杖を突いた男性に背後から衝突し、男性は脳挫傷で重症となった。　自転車の加害者は、前方不注意の過失責任が問われる。　二人乗り自転車、三人乗り自転車は重量があり、歩行者に衝突した場合死亡事故に繋がる。　しかし、杖を突いた歩行者は運動神経が低下しているため、スグに自転車を避けることは、困難であるが、事前に自転車が来ることを知らせていれば、衝突事故は避けられるでしょう。

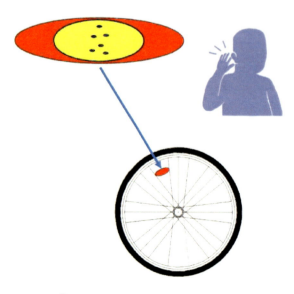

⑶ 車椅子と自転車

　歩道と車道の区別がない道路に於いて、自転車が走行中、前方の車椅子が前から歩いて来る歩行者を避けるため、向きを変えた時に後方の自転車が車椅子に衝突し、車椅子の被害者に重症を負わせた。　急な車椅子の進路変更を予知することが出来ない自転車の加害者には前方不注意の過失責任が問われる。　しかし、車椅子の被害者に後方から自転車が来ることを知らせていれば、衝突事故は避けられるでしょう。

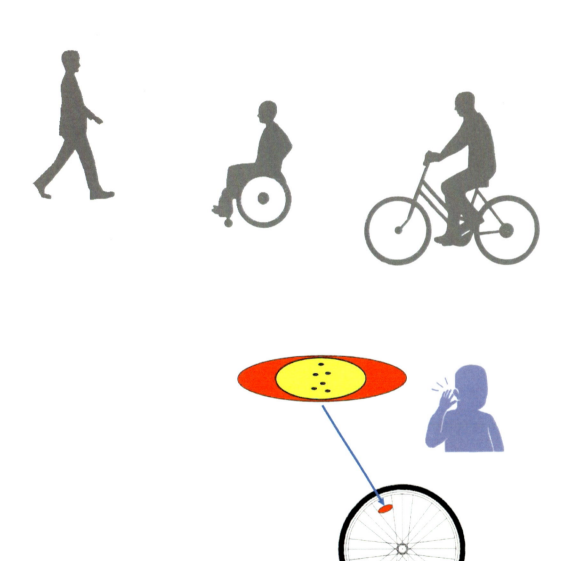

⑷　横断歩道の衝突、歩行者と自転車

　　自転車が信号を無視し、横断歩道の歩行者と衝突。歩行者は脳挫傷で死亡した被害者となり、自転車の加害者は前方不注意の過失責任が問われる。信号点滅の無理な横断による事故が多い。しかし、被害者に自転車が来ることを知らせていれば、衝突事故は避けられるでしょう。

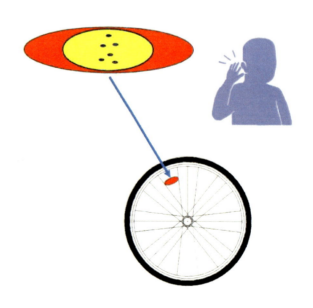

(5) 曲がり角の死角、自転車と自転車

　自転車と自転車の衝突事故の場合、一方の自転車がスピードを落とさないため片方の自転車と衝突した。　片方の自転車が気をつけていても、避けることが出来ない事故ですが、どちらかの自転車に自転車が来ることを音で知らせていれば、衝突事故は避けられるでしょう。

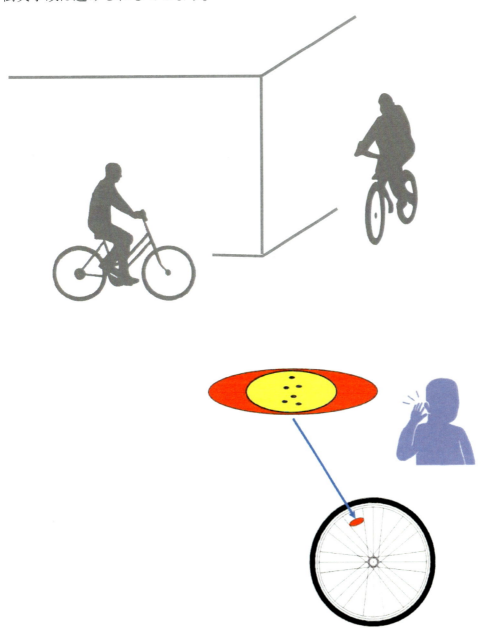

(6) 河川敷、ランナーと自転車

　マラソンをしているランナーに背後から自転車が猛スピードでランナーに衝突、ランナーは河川敷で障害物を避けるために進路を変更した時に自転車に衝突された。　しかし、この時の自転車が来ることを音で知らせていれば事故は回避できるでしょう。

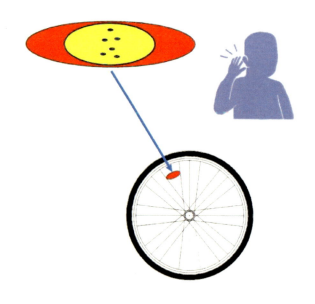

12

2　音と光で知らせる自転車事故防止の表現-

　この自転車用反射版は、夜道に於いて、歩行者に自転車の存在をしらせることができる楕円形の両面の反射板であり、この反射板は、自転車の車輪のスポークの間に取り外し自在にセットすることができる。

　反射板の片方に半円状の空洞を形成し、その空洞の中に鈴を設ける。　この鈴が走行中の車輪の回転により、音を発し、自転車の存在を周囲に知らせる。

　この鈴の音と自転車のスピードの関係においては、自転車が猛スピードで走行中の場合は、車輪の回転数が上がり、鈴の音も高音になり、自転車の存在を広範囲に知らせる事が出来る。　従って、河川敷などでマラソン、ランナーを追い越す場合、自転車の存在を知らせる事ができ、自転車事故が多い河川敷でランナーとの事故防止に役立つ。

　下り坂の自転車の走行でも、スピードが増し、車輪の回転数が上がり、鈴の音も高音になり、歩行者、車椅子、その他などに自転車の存在を知らせることができ、事故防止に役立つ。

　猛スピードのマウンテンバイクには、自転車用反射板を複数個取り付けて、鈴の音を高音にすると、より一層の自転車事故防止が期待できる。

著者　増田　志津江

English description

3

Evasion of the bicycle accident and negligence responsibility

(1)

A road and a bicycle without distinction of a sidewalk and a driveway, and a pedestrian

A bicycle crashed into pedestrians on a sidewalk at night, and pedestrians suffered skull fractures that were unconscious. The perpetrator of the bicycle is held responsible for the negligence of the forward and carelessness. However, in this case, if the presence of the bicycle is informed by the sound, the pedestrian will be able to recognize that the bicycle is coming, avoid the bicycle, and avoid the accident.

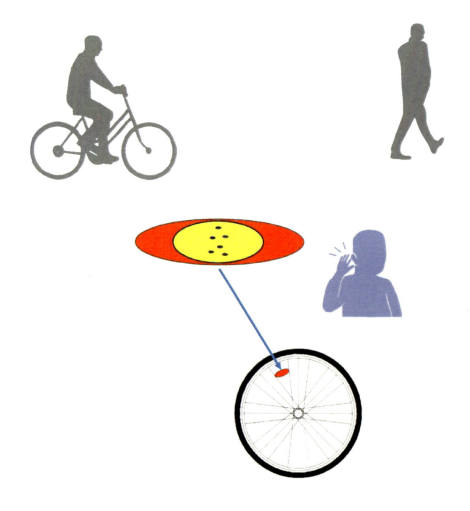

(2)

The pedestrian who poked the two-seater bicycle and the cane

A man has been severely injured with brain contusions after a bicycle carrying a child collided with a man on a walk. The perpetrator of the bicycle is held responsible for the negligence of the forward carelessness. A two-seater bicycle and a three-seater bicycle weigh and can lead to fatal accidents if they collide with pedestrians.

However, pedestrians have reduced reflexes, so it is difficult to avoid bicycles at once, but if you inform them in advance that the bike is coming, you will be able to avoid the collision.

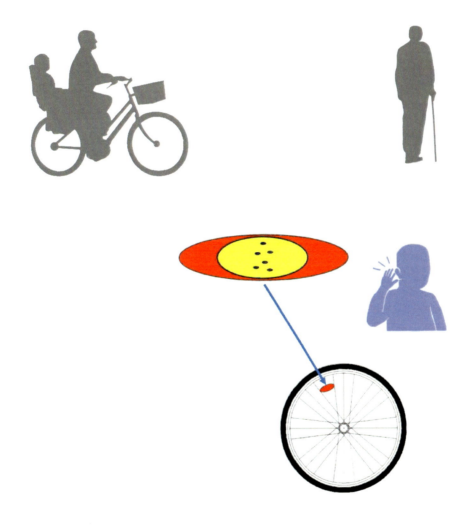

(3)

A wheelchair and a bicycle

On a road where there is no distinction between sidewalks and driveways, when the bicycle is moving and the front wheelchair is moving to avoid pedestrians walking from the front, the rear bike crashed into the wheelchair when it turned around, causing serious damage to the victim of the wheelchair. The perpetrator of the bicycle which cannot foresee a sudden change of course of a wheelchair is held to the responsibility of the negligence of the forward carelessness. However, if you inform the victim of the wheelchair that the bicycle is coming from behind, the collision will be avoided.

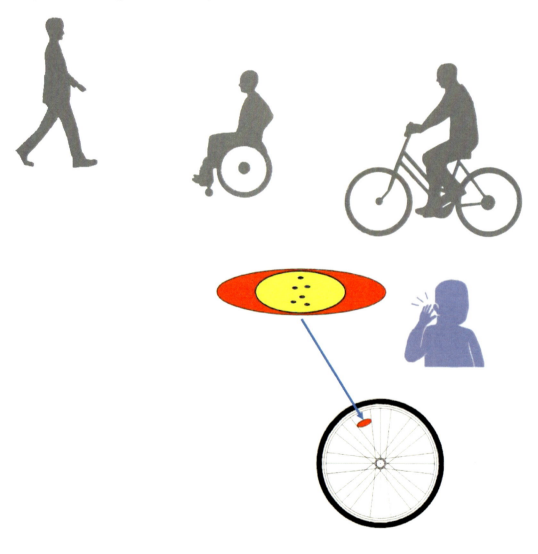

(4)

A collision, pedestrian, and bicycle of a pedestrian crossing

The bicycle ignored the traffic light and collided with pedestrians in the crosswalk. Pedestrians are victims of brain bruising, and the perpetrators of bicycles are held accountable for negligence in the forward. There are a lot of accidents by crossing the signal flashing. However, if the victim is informed that the bicycle is coming, the collision will be avoided.

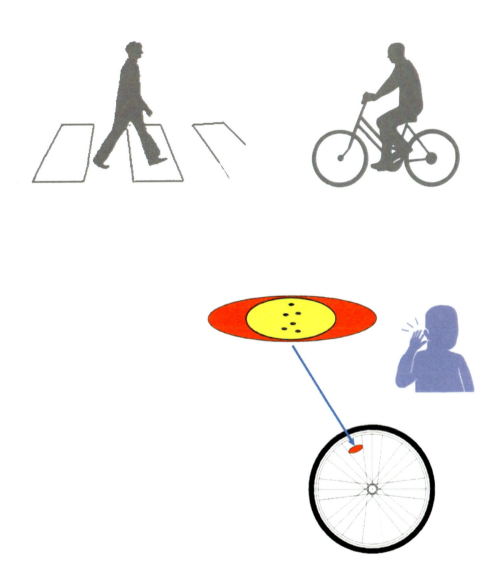

(5)

The dead angle, bicycle, and bicycle of a corner of a street

In the case of a bicycle-to-bike collision, the man's bicycle collided with a female bicycle because it did not slow down.

Even if one bicycle is careful, it is an accident which cannot be avoided,

If you let the sound know that a bicycle is coming on either bike, you will be able to avoid a collision.

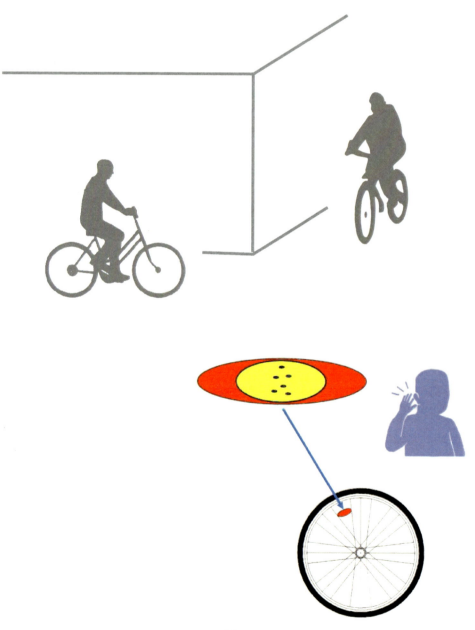

(6)

A dry riverbed, a runner, and a bicycle

An accident that occurred when a marathon runner was hit by a bicycle at a high speed from behind, and the runner changed course to avoid obstacles. However, if the bicycle at this time is informed by the sound, the accident will be avoided.

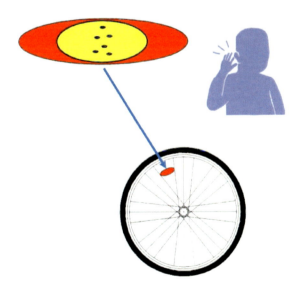

4

Expression of bicycle accident prevention by sound and light

This bicycle reflector can inform pedestrians of the presence of bicycles on the night road.

A circular double-sided reflector, the reflector can be detachably set between the spokes of the bicycle wheel.

A semicircular cavity is formed on one side of the reflector, a bell is provided in the cavity. This bell emits a sound by the rotation of the wheel while running, and informs surroundings of the existence of the bicycle.

In the relationship between the sound of the bell and the speed of the bicycle, when the bicycle is traveling at a high speed, the rotation speed of the wheel goes up, the sound of the bell becomes treble, it is possible to inform the existence of the bicycle extensively. Therefore, when overtaking a marathon or runner in a riverbed, etc., it is possible to inform the presence of a bicycle, it is useful for preventing accidents with runners in the riverbed where there are many bicycle accidents.

Even in the running of the bicycle of the downhill, the speed increases, the rotation speed of the wheel rises, the sound of the bell becomes a treble, and it is possible to inform the presence of the bicycle to the pedestrian and the wheelchair.

If you attach a plurality of bicycle reflectors to a fast mountain bike and make the sound of the bell treble, you can expect even more bicycle accident prevention.

5　公報解説

実用新案登録第 3200491 号
考案の名称；自転車用反射板
実用新案権者；増田　志津江

【要約】
（課題）
外光の不十分な夜道などを自転車で走行するときでも、反射板の機能面、および自転車の走行面での安定性を保ちつつ、確実に自転車の存在を周囲に知らせる自転車用反射板を提供する。

【解決手段】
自転車用反射板２は、片面が外光を反射する反射面２１である２つの部材を、反射面と対向する面で接合して構成される自転車用反射板であって、２つの部材のうち少なくとも一方が膨らみを持つ膨らみ部２５を有し、一方の部材の膨らみ部と他方の部材の間に生ずる空洞２４に、振動により音を生ずる鈴２２を少なくとも一つ備え、２つの部材のうち少なくとも一方には、反射面から空洞まで貫通する貫通穴２３が複数存在し、貫通穴は、鈴よりも十分に小さい、ことを特徴とする。
【選択図】図２

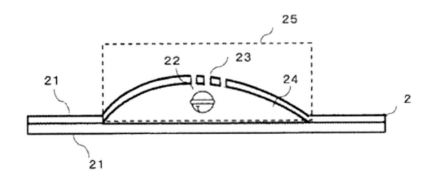

【実用新案登録請求の範囲】
【請求項1】
　片面が外光を反射する反射面である２つの部材を、前記反射面と対向する面で接合して構成される自転車用反射板であって、
　前記２つの部材のうち少なくとも一方が膨らみを持つ膨らみ部を有し、
　一方の部材の前記膨らみ部と他方の部材の間に生ずる空洞に、振動により音を生ずる鈴を少なくとも一つ備え、
　前記２つの部材のうち少なくとも一方には、前記反射面から前記空洞まで貫通する貫通穴が複数存在し、
　前記貫通穴は、前記鈴よりも十分に小さい、
　ことを特徴とする自転車用反射板。

【考案の詳細な説明】
【技術分野】
【０００１】
　本考案は、自転車用反射板に関する。

【背景技術】
【０００２】
　夜道を自転車で走行している際に、自転車の存在を知らせる手段の一つに反射板がある。反射板は主に自転車の車輪のスポーク-スポーク間に設置されている。
　夜道を走行中に、街灯や車のヘッドライトなどの光が反射板に当たると、反射板は光が入射した方向に反射光として光を発する。その反射光により周囲に自転車の存在を気づかせることができる。自転車用の反射板は様々な形状のものが提案されており、例えば特許文献１、特許文献２のようなものがある。

【０００３】
　しかし、夜道に自転車を走行中に、街灯や車による光が必ずしも十分である場面に限らず、光が不十分な場面で、自転車と歩行者がお互いの存在に気付かず接触事故を起こしてしまうケースが多々ある。
　お互いの存在を認識するためには、外光に依存する従来の自転車用の反射板では不十分であるという課題のもと、かかる課題の解決を図った例として非特許文献１がある。

【先行技術文献】
【特許文献】
【０００４】
【特許文献１】　特開２００１－２２５７７２号公報
【特許文献２】　特開平１１－１１５８４８号公報

【非特許文献】
【０００５】
【非特許文献１】奥田裕幸、"レポドラ日記"、[online]、平成26年11月3日、名古屋市名東区、[平成27年7月10日検索]、インターネット、
〈URL：http://blog.hicbc.com/weblog/repodora/2014/11/010970.php〉

【０００６】
　非特許文献１には、光の入射した方向に反射光を発する反射板に鈴を外付けした自転車用の反射板が公開されている。

【考案の概要】
【考案が解決しようとする課題】
【0007】
　しかしながら、非特許文献１の考案では、鈴が剥き出しのため走行中に鈴が取れてしまうといった音で周囲に存在を知らせる機能面での安定性、また車輪のスポーク等含めた自転車の部品、もしくは他の障害物に鈴が引っかかってしまうといった自転車の走行面での安定性に課題がある。

【0008】
　本考案は、上記課題に鑑みてなされたもので、外光の不十分な夜道などを自転車で走行するときでも、反射板の機能面、および自転車の走行面での安定性を保ちつつ、確実に自転車の存在を周囲に知らせる自転車用反射板を提供することを目的とする。

【課題を解決するための手段】
【0009】
　かかる目的を達成するために、本考案にかかる自転車用反射板は、片面が外光を反射する反射面である２つの部材を、反射面と対向する面で接合して構成される自転車用反射板であって、２つの部材のうち少なくとも一方が膨らみを持つ膨らみ部を有し、一方の部材の膨らみ部と他方の部材の間に生ずる空洞に、振動により音を生ずる鈴を少なくとも一つ備え、２つの部材のうち少なくとも一方には、反射面から空洞まで貫通する貫通穴が複数存在し、貫通穴は、鈴よりも十分に小さい、ことを特徴とする。

【考案の効果】
【0010】
　本考案によれば、外光の不十分な夜道などを自転車で走行するときでも、反射板の機能面、および自転車の走行面での安定性を保ちつつ、確実に自転車の存在を周囲に知らせる自転車用反射板を提供することができる。

【図面の簡単な説明】
【0011】
【図1】本考案の実施形態に係る自転車の車輪の外観図である。
【図2】本考案の実施形態に係る反射板の断面図である。
【図3】本考案の実施形態に係る膨らみを持つ反射面の表面図である。
【図4】他の実施例に係る反射板の断面図である。

【考案を実施するための形態】
【0012】
　本考案の実施形態の一例について説明する。
　図1は本考案の実施形態に係る自転車の車輪の外観図である。車輪1は一般的な自転車に備えてある車輪であり、この図に限定されるものではない。車輪1のスポーク-スポーク間に反射板2が備え付けられている。反射板を備え付ける位置としては、この図に限定されず、例えば車輪以外の自転車を構成する部位に備え付けることも可能である。

【0013】
　図2は本考案の実施形態に係る反射板の断面図の一例である。反射板2は光が入射した方向に反射光を発する反射板を想定しており、反射板を構成する材料は金属製や樹脂製、その他の素材でも構わない。片面が反射面21である2つの部材が、反射面21と反対の面同士で互いに接合されている。反射板2を形成する少なくとも一方の部材は空洞24ができるよう膨らんでいる膨らみ部25を有している。一方の部材の膨らみ部と他方の部材の間に生ずる空洞24の内部に振動により音を生ずる鈴22が入っている。また、膨らみ部25の表面には、空洞24まで貫通した複数の貫通穴23がある。尚、貫通穴23は雨水の侵入をできるだけ抑制するため、膨らみ部25の中央部に位置している。空洞24は、鈴22が様々な方向に動くことができるよう、鈴22に対して十分広い領域となっている。

【0014】
　また、図３は本考案の実施形態に係る膨らみを持つ反射面の表面図である。反射面２１の領域内部に膨らみ部２５があり、その膨らみ部２５の表面に貫通穴２３が複数存在する。尚、膨らみ部２５の領域であるが、図３の領域に限定されず、反射板を構成する２つの部材が少なくとも１つの接合面を各々有するように接合されていれば、反射面２１の領域範囲内での変更は可能である。また、接合する２つの部材の間に生ずる隙間（膨らみ部２５内部の空洞２４は除く）の幅は、鈴２２の直径よりも十分に小さい。また膨らみ部２５は、走行面での安定性を保てる程度に十分に突出している。

【0015】
　本考案による反射板を備えた自転車が走行すると、車輪の回転運動により反射板の空洞
内を鈴が動き、音が出る。鈴の音は反射板の表面の貫通穴から周囲の人間にも聞こえる。また、外光が反射面に当たると光を反射して存在を知らせる従来の反射板の機能も備えており、光と音の双方で周囲に自転車の存在を知らせることができる。

【0016】
　また、反射面の貫通穴は鈴に比べて十分に小さく構成される。貫通穴が鈴よりも十分に小さいので貫通穴から鈴が飛び出すということがなく、反射板の機能面、および自転車の走行面でも安定性がある。

【００１７】
　以上、本考案を好適な形態で行う例を説明した。ここでは特定の具体例を示して説明を行ったが、実用新案の範囲の趣旨及び範囲から逸脱しない範囲で、本具体例の様々な修正、および形態、形状の変更などが可能である。例えば、図４に示すように、反射面の膨らみにより生じる空洞への貫通穴を、膨らみ部を持つ反射面と反対の反射面から空けることもできる。また、貫通穴は、部材の中央部に限定されず、部材の反射面の全面に位置するようにしてもよく、貫通穴が鈴より十分に小さく、鈴が外部に飛び出す事態を防ぐことができればそれで十分である。また、反射板を構成する２つの部材の接合状態は、接着剤などで膨らみ部の内部の空洞を除いて隙間無く接着されていてもよく、ネジなどで接合されていてもよい。また、熱溶着などで接着されていてもよく、接合状態はこれに限定されない。

【符号の説明】

【0018】
- 1　　自転車の車輪
- 2　　反射板
- 21　　反射面
- 22　　鈴
- 23　　貫通穴
- 24　　空洞
- 25　　膨らみ部

【図1】

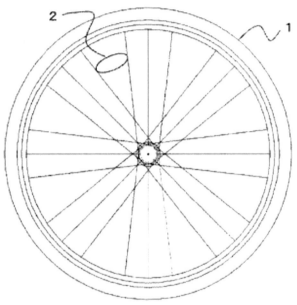

【図2】

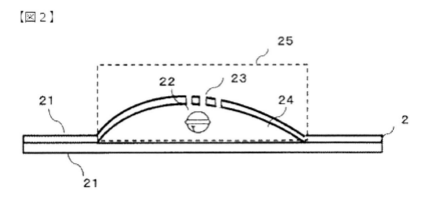

【図3】

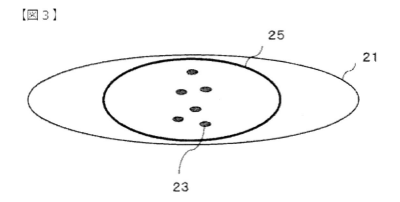

【図4】

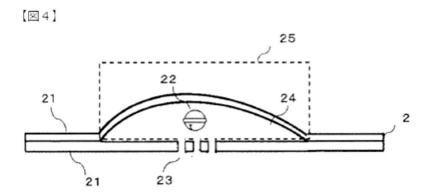

Patent journal English

[Overview] (Modified)

[Problem]

To provide a reflecting plate for a bicycle, which surely informs the surroundings of the existence of a bicycle, while maintaining stability on the functional surface of a reflecting plate and on the running surface of a bicycle, even when an insufficient night or the like of an external light is caused by a bicycle.

[Means for solving]

A reflecting plate 2 for a bicycle is a reflecting plate for a bicycle constituted by joining 2 members, one on one side, which is a reflecting surface 21 for reflecting external light, on a surface opposed to a reflecting surface, and at least one of 2 members has a swollen part 25 with a swelling. At least one bell 22 generating sound due to vibration is provided in a cavity 24 formed between a bulge part of one member and the other member, a plurality of through holes 23 penetrating from a reflection surface to a cavity are provided at least at one of the 2 members, and the through hole is sufficiently smaller than a bell.

[Selected drawing] Fig.2

000002

Scope of Claims

Close

[Utility Model Claims]

[Claim 1]

In this bicycle reflector for a bicycle bicycle, 2 members which are reflecting surfaces for reflecting external light on one side are joined to each other on a surface facing the reflecting surface.

At least one of the 2 members has a bulge with a bulge.

At least one bell which generates sound due to vibration is provided in a cavity generated between the bulging part of one member and the other member.

At least one of the 2 members has a plurality of through holes penetrating from the reflecting surface to the cavity.

The through hole is sufficiently smaller than the bell.

The light reflector for bicycles characterized by things.

Detailed Description

Close

[Detailed description of the device]

[Technical field]

[0001]

This invention relates to a reflector for a bicycle.

[Background of the Invention]

[0002]

A reflector is one of the means for informing the presence of a bicycle when a bicycle is traveling on a bicycle. The reflector is located primarily between the spoke-spokes of the wheels of the bicycle.

When light such as a streetlamp or a vehicle headlight strikes a reflecting plate while traveling on a night road, the reflecting plate emits light as reflected light in the direction in which light is incident. The reflected light makes it possible to remind the surroundings of the presence of a bicycle. Various types of reflecting plates have been proposed for bicycles, and examples thereof include Patent Documents 1 and 2.

[0003]

However, while the bicycle is running in the midnight, there is many cases in which the bicycle and the pedestrian are not aware of the existence of each other and cause a contact accident in a situation where the light is insufficient, not limited to a scene in which light by the streetlamp and the vehicle is always 10 minutes.

In order to recognize the presence of each other, Non-Patent document 1 has been proposed as an example of solving such problems, with the problem that conventional reflecting plates for bicycles relying on external light are insufficient.

[Prior art reference]
[Patent document]
[0004]
[Patent document 1]Japanese Patent Laid-Open No. 225772 2001
[Patent document 2]JP H 11 - 115848A

[Non-patent documents]

[0005]

[Non-patent document1]Okuda **, "**** Diary", [online], November 3, 2014, Nagoya Meito Ward, [Search on Jul. 10, 2015], Internet, & lt ; URL:http://blog.hicbc.com/weblog/repodora/2014/11/010970.php & gt ;.

[0006]

In Non-Patent Document 1, a reflecting plate for a bicycle is disclosed in which a bell is externally attached to a reflecting plate which emits reflected light in a direction in which light is incident.

[Summary of the device]
[Problem to be solved by the device]

[0007]

However, according to the proposal of Non-Patent Document 1, there is a problem in stability on a functional surface which informs the presence of a bell by a sound such that a bell is removed due to exposure, and stability on a running surface of a bicycle, such as a case where a bell is caught by a part of a bicycle or another obstacle including spokes of a wheel.

[0008]

In view of the above problems, it is an object of the present invention to provide a bicycle reflector which is capable of reliably informing the surroundings of the bicycle, while maintaining the stability of the reflecting plate on the function surface and the running surface of the bicycle, even when the vehicle travels in a short night.

[Means for solving the problem]

[0009]

To achieve this object, a reflecting plate for a bicycle according to the present invention is a reflecting plate for a bicycle, wherein one of 2 members, which is a reflecting surface of one side of which reflects external light, is bonded on a surface facing the reflecting surface, and at least one of the 2 members has a bulging portion which has a bulge, and is formed between the bulging portion of one member and the other member. At least one bell which generates sound due to vibration is provided, and a plurality of through holes penetrating from a reflecting surface to a cavity are provided at least at one of 2 members, and the through hole is sufficiently smaller than a bell.

[Effect of the device]

[0010]

According to the present invention, it is possible to provide a bicycle reflector which is capable of reliably informing the surroundings of the bicycle of the presence of a bicycle, while maintaining the function of the reflector and the stability of the bicycle on the running surface, even when the vehicle travels on a short night of the outside light.

[Brief Description of the Drawings]

[0011]

[Fig. 1]FIG. 1 is an external view of a wheel of a bicycle according to an embodiment of the present invention ;.

[Fig. 2]FIG. 1 is a cross-sectional view of a reflector according to an embodiment of the present invention ;.

[Fig. 3]FIG. 4 is a front view of a reflective surface having a bulge according to an embodiment of the present invention ;.

[Fig. 4]FIG. 4 is a cross-sectional view of a reflector according to another embodiment ;.

[Mode for carrying out the device]

[0012]

An example of an embodiment of the present invention will be described.

FIG. 1 is an external view of a wheel of a bicycle according to an embodiment of the present invention. Wheel 1 is a wheel provided in a typical bicycle, and is not limited thereto. A reflector 2 is provided between the spoke-spokes of the wheels 1. The position where the reflector is provided is not limited to this figure, and may be provided, for example, at a portion of a bicycle other than a wheel.

[0013]

FIG. 2 is an example of a cross-sectional view of a reflector according to an embodiment of the present invention. The reflector 2 is assumed to be a reflector which emits reflected light in the direction of incidence of light, and the material of the reflector may be made of metal, resin, or other material. 2 members whose one side is a reflection surface 21 are joined to each other on the opposite side of the reflection surface 21. At least one of the members forming the reflector 2 has a bulge 25 which bulges into a cavity 24. A bell 22 which generates sound by vibration is contained inside a cavity 24 which is formed between a bulge part of one member and the other member. Also, a plurality of through holes 23 are formed in the surface of the bulge 25 and extend through the cavity 24. In addition, the through hole 23 is located at a central portion of the bulge portion 25 in order to suppress intrusion of rainwater as much as possible. Cavity 24 is a sufficiently wide area relative to bell 22 to allow bell 22 to move in various directions.

[0014]

FIG. 3 is a front view of a reflective surface having a bulge according to an embodiment of the present invention. There is a bulge 25 in the area of the reflective surface 21, and a plurality of through holes 23 in the surface of the bulge 25. It should be noted that, although the region of the bulge 25 is not limited to the region of FIG. 3, it is possible to change the region of the reflective surface 21 as long as the 2 members constituting the reflective plate have at least one bonding surface. Also, the width of the gap (excluding the cavity 24 inside the bulge 25) that occurs between the 2 members to be joined is sufficiently smaller than the diameter of the bell 22. Also, the bulge 25 protrudes sufficiently to maintain stability on the running surface.

[0015]

When the bicycle provided with the light reflector by this design runs, it is a cavity of a light reflector by rotational movement of a wheel.

The bell moves and sounds out. Sound of the bell is also heard from the through hole of the surface of the reflector to the surrounding person. Further, it has the function of a conventional reflecting plate which reflects the light when the external light strikes the reflecting surface and informs the presence of the light, and it is possible to inform the surroundings of the bicycle by both of the light and the sound.

[0016]

Further, the through hole of the reflecting surface is sufficiently smaller than that of the bell. Since the through hole is sufficiently smaller than the bell, there is no possibility that the bell jumps out of the through hole, and stability is also provided on the functional surface of the reflecting plate and on the running surface of the bicycle.

[0017]

As described above, an example in which the present invention is performed in a preferred form has been described. While specific embodiments have been shown and described, various modifications and changes in the form and shape of the specific example can be made without departing from the spirit and scope of the practical utility. For example, as shown in FIG. 4, a through-hole into the cavity caused by the bulging of the reflecting surface may be opened from a reflecting surface opposite to the reflecting surface having the bulging portion. Further, the through hole is not limited to a central portion of the member, and may be positioned on an entire surface of the reflective surface of the member, and may be 10 minutes as long as the through hole is sufficiently smaller than the bell and the bell is ejected to the outside. In addition, the bonding state of the 2 members constituting the reflecting plate may be bonded without any gap except for a cavity inside the swelling portion with an adhesive or the like, or may be bonded with a screw or the like. Further, it may be bonded by heat welding or the like, and the bonding state is not limited thereto.

[Explanation of letters or numerals]

[0018]

1 bicycle wheel

2 Light Reflector

21 reflective surface

22 bell

23 through hole

24 cavity

25 bulge

[FIG.1]

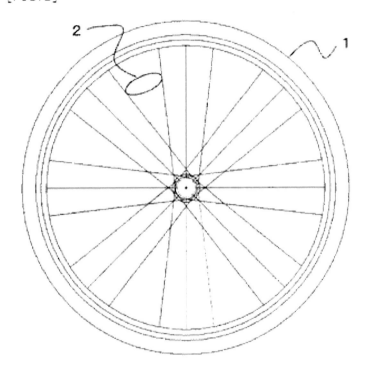

[FIG.2]

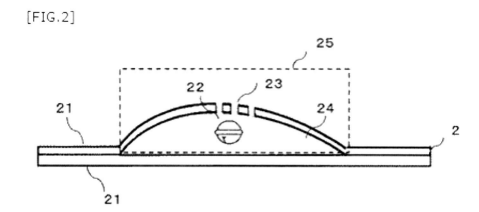

[FIG.3]

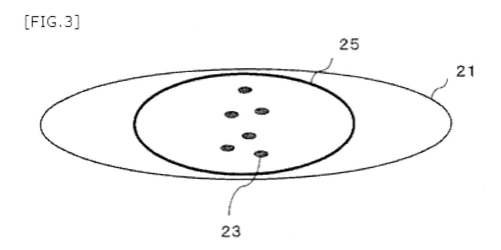

[FIG.4]

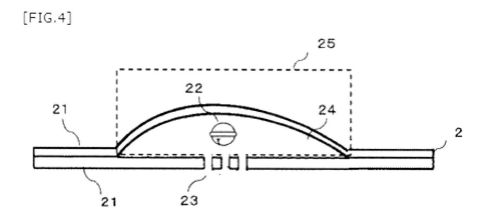

7

        本書の奥付の発行№.について
        №が記載された剥離紙が、枠内に貼られ
        角印が押されている。従って、これが複
        写された本書は、内容が異なる海賊版で
        ありますからご注意ください。

        About issue [of the colophon of this book] №
The angle mark is stamped on the seal with which № was indicated.
Therefore, since this book with which this was copied is a pirate edition from which the contents differ, it should be careful.

8

過失責任軽減の主張マニュアル

前方不注意とされる判断、音を発した自転車の過失責任軽減の主張マニュアル
マニュアルの詳細については、奥付の発行№.と購入先をメールでお知らせ下さい。

The opinion manual of negligence responsibility mitigation
Forward careless judgment, claims manual of negligence liability reduction of the bicycle that emits sound
For more information on the manual, please email the imprint date, number, and place of purchase.

音で知らせる自転車反射板　自転車事故・過失軽減

定価（本体 3,800 円＋税）

２０１９年（令和元年）８月５日発行

No.  MSD04-7-025

発行所　IDF（INVENTION DEVLOPMENT FEDERATION）

発明開発連合会®

メール 03-3498@idf-0751.com　www.idf-0751.com

電話 03-3498-0751㈹

150-8691 渋谷郵便局私書箱第２５８号

発行人　ましば寿一

著作権企画　IDF 発明開発(連)©

Printed in Japan

著者　増田　志津江

※宣伝・説明・明細書表現などへの引用を禁止。
The quotation to advertisement, explanation, specification expression, etc. is forbidden.
本書の一部または全部を無断で複写、複製、転載、データーファイル化することを禁じています。
It forbids a copy, a duplicate, reproduction, and forming a data file for some or all of this book without notice.